SALES SUCCESS SECRETS

TURNING PROSPECT INTO THANKFUL CLIENT

BY

KATHY R. ORRELL

Copyright © [2024] by [KATHY R ORRELL]

All rights reserved. No part of this publication may be reproduced, distributed, or transmitted in any form or by any means, including photocopying, recording, or other electronic or mechanical methods, without the prior written permission of the publisher, except in the case of brief quotations embodied in critical reviews and certain other noncommercial uses permitted by copyright law.

DISCLIAMER

The techniques in this book are meant to maximise your financial potential. Personal financial decisions are complicated and particular to each person, though. The counsel in this book is meant to be informative and instructive; it is not to be regarded as professional, legal, or financial advice. Before making any financial decisions, please speak with a licenced expert.

ACKNOWLEDGEMENT

Writing this book has been a path of development, learning, and introspection; without the help, inspiration, and direction of many people it would not have been possible.

First and most importantly, I want to thank my family for their consistent support and encouragement along this process. My strength has come mostly from your belief in me. Thank you for your love and support, to my rock—who has been there for me—offering patience and understanding over the many hours spent writing. Thank you for reminding my children—who have been my main inspiration—of the value of tenacity and commitment.

I owe Richard Donovan a great deal as his real-life sales expertise and guidance have greatly shaped the course of this book. My perspective of what it really means to be successful in sales was much shaped by your insights into the art of modern sales and your focus on developing real relationships with customers. I am always grateful for the knowledge and insight you have given me; your mentoring has been really priceless.

I also like to thank Taylor A. Welch for her efforts; her book *"Winning at Sales* inspired my own research in the sales field. Your focus on the need of offering value and developing long-term bonds with clients gave me a basis from which I could develop and widen my concepts. Your work has motivated me to consider more closely the part empathy, understanding, and ongoing sales improvement play.

My sales sector colleagues and peers deserve a particular thank you for their experiences and insights, which have enhanced my awareness of the opportunities and difficulties we now confront. Helping me to hone the ideas provided in this book has been much aided by your eagerness to share your knowledge, debate ideas, and provide helpful criticism.

I also like to thank my editor; her sharp eye and intelligent recommendations have helped me hone and improve this work. I really appreciate your contributions as your commitment to excellence and meticulousness have improved this book.

Finally, thank you to all the salespeople and thought leaders whose work has shaped my perspective—books, podcasts, essays, or personal interactions. Two ongoing sources of motivation have been your dedication to ongoing improvement and your love of the sales craft. In many respects, this book is an homage to the cumulative knowledge of those who have come before me and those who keep stretching the bounds of what is feasible in the sales sphere.

Without all of your help and inspiration, this book would not have been feasible. We appreciate your donations, support, and conviction in the value of knowledge and personal development. I owe each and every one of you great gratitude.

Contents

INTRODUCTION 2

The Sales Revolution: An Exploration of the New Selling Landscape 2

The New Age of Sales 10

CHAPTER ONE 14

Understanding Your Customer 14

CHAPTER TWO 23

Building Genuine Connections.................... 23

ESTABLISHING SINCERE RELATIONSHIP ... 30

CHAPTER THREE 40

Creating Your Value Proposition 40

CHAPTER FOUR 50

Strategies for Effective Communication 50

CHAPTER FIVE 57

Using Psychology to Improve Sales............... 57

CHAPTER SIX 64

Managing Disagreements with Self-Assurance 64

CHAPTER SEVEN 70

Developing a Customer-Centric Sales Strategy 70

CHAPTER EIGHT 79

The Value of Further Investigation 79

CHAPTER NINE 86

Creating Advocates Out of Clients 86

CHAPTER TEN 93

Sales Improvement That Never Stops 93

INTRODUCTION

The Sales Revolution: An Exploration of the New Selling Landscape

The Chronicles of a Reluctant Salesman

John Harper entered Dynamics Corp.'s main office early in October, a cool morning. His heart raced, his hands were moist, and a knot developed in his gut. John did not make his living selling. Actually, he had always felt himself as everything but. He was a product engineer a year ago, working in a quiet area of the office inventing and refining creative ideas. But as life sometimes happens, it had different ideas.

The business was in a difficult situation; revenues were declining and layoffs were almost sure. Knowing John's great knowledge of the items, his manager had urged him to move into a sales post—a request more akin to a directive. John loved the company and the items he helped produce; it was simply that sales had always been a mystery to him—a world of slick talkers, limitless goals, and constant pressure. He had no wish to enter this planet.

Here he was, nonetheless, preparing to start his new position outside Richard Donovan's Vice President of Sales office. John met Richard with a solid handshake and a kind smile as the door opened. John, welcome to the team. Though I know this is a significant adjustment for you, believe me—you have what it takes—that seems to discount any uncertainty.

John pushed a smile, but his mind ran wild with doubt. He had no official sales training, no closing deal experience, and no ambition to participate in what he considered to be the craft of persuasion. Still, he felt he had little option as he left Richard's office. Along with a mortgage to pay, he had family to maintain and a company depending on him.

A Different Viewpoint on the New Era of Sales

John's trip across the sales landscape over the next several months was a rollercoaster of emotions, mistakes, and little triumphs. He soon came to see that his preconceptions about sales were out of current and, in many respects, totally incorrect. Sales was about knowing people, developing relationships, and offering value, not only about persuading someone to buy a good.

John sat down with Richard for a heart-to--heart one day following yet another demanding conference with a possible client that concluded with a "We'll think about it," John said, "I just feel I'm not cut out for this." Not a salesman, but an engineer here.

Richard slanted back in his chair and gazed carefully at John. "John, you are thinking about this all backwards. You are solving problems, not only marketing a good. You are providing remedies that improve the quality of people's life. It's more about knowing the client and delivering actual value than about the pitch. Modern sales is all about exactly this. Nowadays, the clever sell is rather important than the hard sell.

John really related to those words. Richard was talking about something far deeper than sales, something that connected with his own principles, while he had always considered sales as a transactional procedure. Sales was about connection, knowledge, and service, not about pressure or manipulation. It was about fostering relationships that endured and confidence.

John started to change in viewpoint. As an engineer, he began to view sales as an expansion of his always problem-solving nature. He started paying closer attention, asking better questions, and emphasizing the wants of the consumer above the product's attributes. Things started to alter, slow but definitely. Deals started closing, clients behaved differently, and John discovered he was not only reaching but beyond his goals.

The Selling Revolution

John Harper's narrative is not singular. In the realm of sales, a silent revolution is under progress worldwide and in many different sectors. A new approach that gives empathy, understanding, and long-term relationships top priority is replacing the traditional hard selling, cold calling, and high-pressure techniques.

This book explores that revolution. It's about the change from pushing for a speedy close to developing lifelong client relationships from selling goods to solving problems. It's about using psychology, statistics, and technology to produce more intelligent, successful sales plans. Most essential, it's about realizing that the most effective salesmen of today are those who listen the best rather than the loudest ones.

The truth is, the planet has evolved. Consumers now are more informed, more empowered, and more discriminating than they were a few years ago They want to be understood; they do not want sold to. They desire to do business with people that really concern their wants and who are dedicated to enable them to reach their objectives. Sales in this new age need for a different type of salesman—one who is part advisor, part problem-solver, and part trusted partner.

The Science and Artistry of Sales

Integration of art and science has been one of the most important developments in the sales scene. Although sales have long been considered as an art—an instinctive process grounded on personal interactions and relationships—it is also becoming a science more and more. Helping salespeople better understand their clients, forecast results, and maximize their plans now depends critically on data, analytics, and technology.

Sales success used to be sometimes ascribed to gut feeling, personality, and charm. Though these traits are still vital today, a data-driven strategy that offers insightful analysis of consumer behavior, market trends, and sales performance balances them. The contemporary salesperson is a strategist, a storyteller, and an analyst—a relationship builder as well.

This book will walk you through the fundamental abilities

and tactics required to thrive in this new sales age. You will learn how to create real relationships with your clients, how to use data to guide wiser decisions, and how to create value propositions that appeal to buyers of today. You will learn how to clearly express yourself, confidently address challenges, and transform consumers into advocates pushing recommendations and recurring business.

Why This Book?

You could be asking why you ought to pick up this book. After all, there are several books on sales, all promising to reveal the keys of success. What therefore distinguishes this one from others?

First, this book is based on the actual experiences of salespeople who have negotiated the difficulties of the current market. It's not just theory or abstract ideas; it's useful, doable guidance you can start right now for your own sales initiatives.

Second, this book admits the subtleties and complexity of contemporary sales. It's not about providing one-size-fits-all cures or short cuts. Rather, it offers a thorough framework for analyzing the several facets of sales, from consumer psychology to data analytics, and how they interact to produce a winning plan.

Third, this book covers more ground than merely terminating business. It's about launching a happy, sustainable, and profitable career in sales. It's about honing the abilities and attitude required to succeed in a fast changing environment where the only constant is change.

At last, this book is written from your perspective. This book is meant to meet you where you are and enable you to go to where you want to be, regardless of your level of sales experience or newness like John Harper was.

The Path Forward

You will set off a voyage of inquiry as you turn through this book. You will learn from top performers, investigate the newest sales trends and best practices, and get ideas on how you could always be improving and adjusting to new conditions.

But this path is about doing as much as studying. Every chapter is meant to provide you useful tools and techniques to apply in your regular job. This book addresses all the key components of effective selling from knowing your consumer to developing real connections, creating your value proposition, and learning the art of follow-up.

You will also explore more complex subjects include using psychology in sales, confidently addressing challenges, and developing a client-centric strategy that centers the client in all you do. Along the road, you will learn how to build a culture of ongoing development inside your sales force and how to convert clients into advocates who actively promote your goods and services.

Applying these techniques will start to show results not only in your sales figures but also in the connections you create, the confidence you develop, and the gratification you get from your work. Sales is not only a job; it's a trade, a career, and, when done correctly, a very fulfilling endeavor.

A Fresh Approach for a New Age

This book is really about attitude at its essence. In the modern world, the most effective salespeople are those that approach their business with a growth mindset—that is, a belief that their talents and abilities can be developed by commitment and hard effort. Curious, flexible, and constantly seeking for means of development.

Success in this new sales era is more about your ability to understand and service your clients than about who you know. It's about generating value and developing enduring relationships, not about sealing the business at all at costs. It's about solving problems and having a positive influence rather than about pushing a product.

I advise you to develop this attitude as you go through the next chapters. Open to fresh ideas, ready to question your presumptions, and ready to welcome the changes transforming the sales scene. Whether you are just starting out or a seasoned sales professional, there is always more to learn, uncover, and ways to develop.

Final Thought: Starting Here

Your Transformational Sales

Sales is a field undergoing transformation right now. New techniques more customer-centric, data-driven, and relationship-oriented are replacing the conventional ways of doing things. Your road map for negotiating this shifting terrain and flourishing in the new sales age is this book.

Turning the pages and delving into the chapters that lie ahead will equip you with the tools, techniques, and insights you need to succeed. Sales is not only a job, but a voyage of constant learning, development, and improvement as well.

Ready then to start your own sales revolution? Are you ready to change your perspective on sales, deepen your relationships with your clients, and realize the success you have always wanted? If yes, this book is meant for you.

Welcome into the next sales age. Allow us to begin.

The New Age of Sales

Over the past few decades, there has been a significant transformation in the sales landscape. The days of forceful sales pitches and hard sells are long gone. These days, the emphasis is on providing value, comprehending the needs of the consumer, and developing real relationships. Greetings from the modern sales period, when customers purchase experiences, trust, and solutions in addition to goods. This chapter delves into this change, examining the reasons for the evolution of sales and what it implies for you as a sales professional.

The Transition in Sales from Transactional to Relational

Sales used to be frequently thought of as a transactional process. The objective was uncomplicated: close the deal, move on to the next client. But rather of cultivating a loyal customer base over time, this strategy frequently resulted in a one-time sale. Successful salespeople nowadays are aware that establishing lasting relationships is essential. A Bain & Company study found that a 5% improvement in client retention rates results in a 25% to 95% increase in earnings. This emphasizes the value of fostering connections as opposed to concentrating only on one-time deals.

The Value of Authenticity and Trust

In today's sales landscape, trust is critical. According to an Edelman study, 81% of consumers agree that a brand's ability to earn their trust influences their decision to buy. Transparency and authenticity are now required; they are no longer optional. Thanks to social media and the internet, consumers have access to more information than ever before. They are quick to avoid companies or salespeople that don't seem sincere since they can tell when someone is being dishonest. Being truthful about the capabilities of your product, accepting its limitations, and consistently fulfilling your commitments are all necessary to establish trust.

Making Use of Data and Technology

Many technologies and a wealth of data have been made available by the digital age, which can improve the sales process. Sales personnel can manage prospects, track customer interactions, and customize communications with the use of Customer Relationship Management (CRM) tools. Salesforce reports that businesses using CRM systems receive a 29% average boost in sales. Furthermore, data analytics can reveal information about the preferences, behavior, and pain areas of customers, allowing salespeople to better target their approaches and present more pertinent solutions.

Social Selling's Ascent

Social media has developed into a potent weapon in the sales toolbox. Social media sites like Instagram, Twitter, and LinkedIn are essential for sales as well as marketing. Using social media to find prospects, cultivate connections, and eventually increase sales is known as social selling. According to a LinkedIn analysis, peers with lower Social

Selling Index scores create 45% less possibilities than social selling leaders. Salespeople may develop their own brands and position themselves as reliable advisors by offering insightful material, interacting with potential customers, and showing their knowledge.

Customer-First Strategy in Sales

A defining characteristic of the new sales age is placing the consumer at the center of the sales process. This entails being aware of their objectives, problems, and needs in order to position your good or service as a remedy. 76% of consumers, according to a Hub Spot survey, believe that businesses should be aware of their wants and expectations. Actively listening to customers, posing pertinent queries, and offering customized solutions are all components of a customer-centric strategy. It involves switching from a generalized, one-size-fits-all strategy to a more individualized, consultative one.

Content Marketing's Power

In the modern sales environment, content marketing is essential. Creating useful and valuable material contributes to authority and trust establishment. Demand Metric estimates that content marketing produces almost three times as many leads at a cost that is 62% lower than traditional marketing. Whitepapers, webinars, case studies, and blogs can instruct prospective customers and direct them through the sales funnel. Content marketing can draw in and develop prospects, eventually resulting in sales, by addressing common problems and providing solutions.

Why Emotional Intelligence Is Important

The importance of emotional intelligence (EI) as a successful sales tool is becoming more widely acknowledged. Emotional intelligence (EI) is the capacity to comprehend and control both your own and other people's feelings. Ninety percent of successful performers have excellent emotional intelligence, according to a Talent Smart research. This translates to sales as having empathy, recognizing nonverbal clues, and reacting suitably to client emotions. Developing close emotional bonds with customers can result in longer-lasting partnerships and increased loyalty.
Ongoing Education and Adjustment

The modern sales environment necessitates ongoing learning and adjustment. The landscape of sales is ever-changing due to the frequent emergence of new technologies, tactics, and consumer habits. Those that are observant, seek out new information, and adjust to changes become good salespeople. This could entail looking for mentorship, reading trade journals, or attending workshops. Maintaining your edge and adding value for your clients is ensured by a dedication to lifelong learning.

CHAPTER ONE

Understanding Your Customer

Successful sales start with a thorough understanding of your customer. We will examine different methods for learning about the requirements and preferences of our customers, examine the significance of customer understanding, and talk about how to use this knowledge to forge closer bonds with customers and increase sales in this chapter.

The Significance of Knowing Your Client

Merely having the demographic information about your consumers is insufficient in today's cutthroat industry. You must comprehend their actions, intentions, difficulties, and goals. With this in-depth knowledge, you can better target your marketing efforts, develop messages that are more pertinent to their needs, and offer solutions that really satisfy them.

Developing a Relationship and Trust Customers are more inclined to conduct business with organizations they trust. PwC found that 43% of consumers would pay more for increased convenience and 42% would pay more for a warm, welcoming environment. Long-term relationships require rapport and trust, both of which are developed when you demonstrate an understanding of your clientele.

Improving Customer Experience You can design individualized experiences if you have a thorough understanding of your customers. According to Epsilon research, when brands provide tailored experiences, 80% of consumers are more inclined to make a purchase. Personalization improves the client experience in general and can take many forms, from specialized product recommendations to customized marketing communications.

Increasing Customer Retention Recognizing and resolving customer pain issues is facilitated by a thorough understanding of your clients. This increases customer retention while simultaneously raising satisfaction levels. According to a Bain & Company study, profitability can rise by 25% to 95% with a 5% increase in client retention.

Methods for Gaining Understanding of Your Client

Both quantitative and qualitative research are necessary to develop a thorough understanding of your clientele. These are a few efficient methods:

Surveys and Questionnaires One direct method of obtaining consumer data is through the administration of surveys and questionnaires. Inquire about their requirements, preferences, and past interactions with your good or service. This approach can be facilitated by using tools like Google Forms or SurveyMonkey.

Interviews with customers Having one-on-one

discussions with clients yields rich, qualitative information. These interviews provide you the chance to learn more about particular problems in-depth, comprehend the background of their actions, and obtain thorough input.

Social Media Listening: There are a wealth of consumer insights available on social media platforms. You may spot trends, attitudes, and possible areas for development by keeping an eye on what consumers are saying about your company and the sector. For social media listening, programs like Brandwatch and Hootsuite can be useful.

Customer Journey Mapping: Creating a map of the customer journey can assist you in comprehending the different points of contact and exchanges that consumers have with your company. This can identify problems and chances to improve the clientele's experience. There are several stages to the journey, including awareness, contemplation, purchase, and post-purchase.

Analyzing Customer Data Make use of data analytics to extract knowledge from customer information. Patterns and trends can be found via purchase histories, CRM systems, and website analytics. For instance, you can determine your best-selling items, peak purchasing periods, and client preferences by examining purchase data.

Comments and Reviews**: What clients like and hate about your product or service can be found out a great deal through online reviews and feedback forms. To learn about customer expectations and potential areas for growth, pay attention to both positive and negative feedback.

Utilizing Customer Data

The next stage is to put this knowledge to use by enhancing your sales approach and customer interactions after you've collected and examined consumer insights.

Personalized Communication Make use of the insights to make your consumer communications more unique. Personalized emails increase conversions by 10% and click-through rates by 14% on average, claims HubSpot. Refer to previous exchanges with clients by name, personalize communications to their interests, and address them by name.

Customized Solutions By being aware of your clients' demands, you can provide solutions that are made especially to relieve their problems. This raises the possibility of a sale and improves client happiness. If a customer regularly buys a particular kind of goods, for example, you might suggest related products that enhance their purchase.

Better Product Development Innovation and product development can be guided by customer input. You may decide on product additions, enhancements, and new services with knowledge about what customers like and dislike. This guarantees that your items suit the requirements and tastes of your customers.

Enhanced Customer Service Assist your customers by providing your team with the knowledge that your study has shown. This helps them to offer more knowledgeable and sympathetic assistance. Customer service is a major consideration for 90% of Americans when choosing a business to do business with, according to Microsoft.

Segmentation and Targeting Make targeted marketing campaigns by segmenting your audience based on consumer data. This enhances the efficacy of your marketing initiatives by enabling you to cater to the particular needs of various customer segments. You can divide up your clientele, for instance, according to their demographics, involvement levels, or past purchases.

An Analysis of Apple's Customer-Centric Strategy

Apple exemplifies a business that thrives in comprehending its clientele. Apple has succeeded not only because of its cutting-edge products but also because of its in-depth knowledge of the wants and demands of its customers. In order to better understand consumer preferences and pain concerns, Apple carries out a lot of research, which influences its marketing and product development initiatives.

For example, Apple recognizes that customers enjoy simplicity and user-friendliness, which is why it prioritizes these features. Apple has developed a devoted following of customers and seen great success by continuously producing goods that both meet and beyond consumer expectations.

Innovative Methods to Increase Client Understanding

Behavioral Analysis, Tracking User Behavior You may

monitor how users engage with your website or app by using tools such as Google Analytics or Hotjar. This covers the pages they visit, their duration of stay, and their point of drop-off. The customer journey's weak points and potential development areas are highlighted by this data.
Heatmaps Heat map tools allow you to see where visitors click on your website the most, giving you information about what attracts visitors' attention and how to improve page layouts for a better user experience.

Customer Segmentation , Psychographic Segmentation Go beyond demographics to divide up your audience according to psychological characteristics including attitudes, values, interests, and lifestyles. This makes tailored messages and more accurate targeting possible.
-**Behavioral Segmentation** Assemble client groups according to their purchasing patterns, product usage patterns, and brand loyalty. Adapt your marketing tactics to these particular ways of being.

Voice of the Customer (VoC) Programs,VoC Surveys Use VoC surveys to speak with customers directly about their expectations, experiences, and recommendations. This procedure can be aided by programs like Medallia and Qualtrics.
- **Net Promoter Score (NPS)** By inquiring about the likelihood that a consumer will refer your good or service, NPS surveys assist in quantifying client loyalty. This measure offers a clear picture of consumer happiness and areas that require improvement.

Advisory Boards for Customers, Establishing Advisory Boards Assemble advisory boards for customers made up of important clients who are able to offer ongoing input and analysis. By doing this, you may maintain a closer relationship and be aware of the needs of your most significant clients.

Partnership Initiatives Meet, talk, and provide feedback to these advisory boards on a regular basis. Their opinions can influence marketing plans, new product development, and customer care initiatives.

Examples of Real-World Customer Understanding

The Personalized Recommendations feature of Amazon's Customer-Centric Model is based on the analysis of browsing and purchasing patterns by means of sophisticated algorithms. Its sales growth and client retention have both benefited greatly from this.

Customer Reviews By emphasizing ratings and reviews from consumers, Amazon helps users make wise choices. Repeat business is encouraged and confidence is increased by this openness.

The Data-Driven Approach of Netflix: - Content Personalization Netflix uses watching data to make personalized movie and show recommendations. Users remain interested and subscribed thanks to this tailored experience.

Predictive Analytics Netflix makes use of predictive analytics to pinpoint trends and inclinations, which directs the production and procurement of content. As a result, there will always be content that appeals to its audience.

Nike is committed to building a community. As such, it offers tailored fitness recommendations, unique merchandise, and early access to new releases. Customers'

sense of community and loyalty are fostered by this program.
Customer Involvement To make sure new goods live up to customer expectations and needs, Nike frequently incorporates customers in the feedback and testing phases of product development.

Using Technology to Improve Understanding of Customers

Machine Learning and Artificial Intelligence (AI): - Predictive Modeling****: AI and machine learning algorithms are able to evaluate large volumes of data in order to forecast the behavior and preferences of customers. This makes tailored experiences and proactive marketing possible.
Chatbots and Virtual Assistants**: AI-driven chatbots collect feedback, offer immediate customer service, and examine interactions to learn about the wants and needs of users.
Customer Data Platforms (CDPs), Unified Customer Profiles, CDPs mix data from several sources to provide thorough customer profiles. More precise targeting and tailored messages are made possible by this comprehensive perspective.
Real-Time Data Processing : This allows CDPs to react quickly to client actions and preferences by processing data in real-time. By doing this, you can be sure that your interactions are current and relevant.

Building a Culture Focused on the Customer

Training and Empowerment for Employees- Customer

Empathy Training**: Teach staff members how to comprehend and relate to customers. This could enhance communication and promote an organization-wide customer-centric attitude.
- **Empowerment Programs**: Provide workers the authority to decide in the best interests of the client. Higher satisfaction and loyalty result from employees feeling empowered to solve problems and improve client experiences.

Customer Satisfaction (CSAT) Evaluate customer satisfaction on a regular basis to determine areas for improvement and assess level of satisfaction.
Assess the ease with which customers may interact with your business and address concerns by using the Customer Effort Score (CES) Customer happiness and loyalty can be considerably increased by lowering effort.

Collaboration Across Functional Lines: - Interdepartmental Communication Promote cooperation across the teams in charge of product development, sales, marketing, and customer support. A coherent strategy for satisfying customer needs is ensured by sharing customer information between departments.
-Combined Techniques Create integrated strategies in line with the objectives of customer-centric thinking. Marketing initiatives must to take into account the information obtained from customer service encounters, for example.

CHAPTER TWO

Building Genuine Connections

In the realm of sales, developing sincere relationships with clients is critical. Successful salespeople are distinguished by their ability to establish a personal connection with customers in a time when they are constantly exposed to a barrage of marketing messages and sales pitches. The significance of genuine relationships, methods for establishing them, and their effect on sustained sales success are all covered in this chapter.

The Value of Sincere Relationships

Foundation of Trust: Trust is the cornerstone of any meaningful connection, and this is particularly true in the sales industry. Trust also fosters loyalty. In a recent Edelman study, 81% of consumers stated that a brand's ability to build trust is what makes or breaks their choice to buy.
- **Loyalty of Customers**: Sincere relationships encourage loyalty. Clients are more inclined to come back when they feel appreciated and understood. According to a Harvard Business Review analysis, clients with strong emotional connections have a twice as high lifetime value as highly happy customers.

Enhanced Customer Experience: - Personal Touch**: Memorable experiences are shaped by one-on-one contact. When a brand feels personal to them, customers are more

inclined to promote it and have favorable opinions about it. 73% of consumers cite the importance of the customer experience in their purchasing decisions, according to PwC research.
- **Tailored Solutions**: By addressing certain wants and preferences, more individualized solutions are possible when there is a greater understanding of the consumer. The overall consumer experience and satisfaction are improved by this personalization.

Enhanced Revenue and Referrals : greater Conversion Rates: Salespeople who establish sincere connections with their customers frequently have greater conversion rates. According to a LinkedIn survey, 78% of sales professionals who employ relationship-building social selling strategies outsell their counterparts who don't.
Word-of-mouth and referrals : Contented clients are more inclined to recommend others. 92% of consumers, according to Nielsen, place more trust in recommendations from friends and family than in other types of promotion.

Methods for Establishing Sincere Relationships

Active Listening , Engagement and Empathy: Active listening entails understanding the needs of the consumer, demonstrating empathy, and giving your complete attention to them. This entails posing open-ended queries and paying attention to the responses without interjecting.
Body Language**: You can show that you are paying attention and are interested in what the customer is saying by leaning in, nodding, and maintaining eye contact.

Personalized Communication - Using Names : Referring to clients by name adds a human element. The well-known quote from Dale Carnegie reads, "A person's name is to that person the sweetest sound in any language."
Personalized Communications : Tailor your message to the customer's interests and previous exchanges. Sending someone a personalized email or message demonstrates your appreciation for them and their unique demands.

Constructing a rapport : Common Ground**: To establish a rapport, look for shared experiences or interests. Talking about a common interest or leaving a remark on a mutual connection on LinkedIn can do this.
Veracity : In your interactions, be sincere. Insincerity can be quickly detected by customers, which damages trust. Authenticity strengthens relationships and increases credibility.

Follow-Up and Consistency : Timely Follow-Ups**: Following a first meeting or sale, get in touch as soon as possible to let the customer know you're interested in their business and are available for any additional help. As per InsideSales.com, half of purchasers select the supplier who gets back to them first.
Consistent Engagement**: Communicate with your clients on a regular basis via phone calls, emails, and social media. Being consistent shows that you are a trustworthy partner who is interested in the relationship.

Adding Value : Educational Content**: Provide useful data and materials that speak to the needs and problems of the client. Whitepapers, webinars, or blog postings could be used for this.

Problem-Solving**: Put the needs of the customer first rather than just selling them stuff. By doing this, you establish yourself as a reliable consultant as opposed to a salesman.

Using Social Media : Professional Networking : Make connections with possible clients by sharing pertinent content on sites like LinkedIn. Social selling is more than simply product promotion; it's about creating relationships. Interesting Content**: Disseminate updates, articles, and insights that benefit your network. Creating interesting material makes you seem knowledgeable and relevant.

Examples of Real-World Relationship Building

Zappos' Superb Customer Service: - **Customer-Centric Approach**: Zappos is well-known for its exceptional customer service, with a corporate culture that places a strong emphasis on establishing sincere relationships. Their agents are taught to establish a rapport and guarantee customer pleasure by spending as much time as necessary on the phone.
- **Surprising and Delightful**: Zappos frequently goes above and above to make a lasting impression and encourage loyalty by sending thank-you letters or upgrading shipping for devoted customers.

Personal Touch from Southwest Airlines: - Introducing Flight Attendants : The airline welcomes its flight attendants to bring personality to their work, whether through lighthearted safety announcements or direct conversations with customers. This strategy produces a satisfying and unforgettable experience.

Customer Recognition : Handwritten notes or shout-outs during flights are just a couple of the unique ways Southwest regularly recognizes and honors its loyal customers.

Community Building at Starbucks: personalized Experience**: Baristas are taught to recall regular customers' orders and to learn and utilize their names. This intimate touch makes the place feel comfortable and familiar.
Customer Engagement**: Starbucks fosters a strong feeling of community and connection with its patrons by interacting with them on social media, organizing community events, and offering loyalty programs.
Sincere Relationships' Effect on Long-Term Success

Customer Advocacy : Brand Ambassadors: genuinely attached customers frequently act as a brand's evangelists. They aggressively spread the word about the business to others in addition to making recurring purchases.
Favorable Testimonials**: Sincere relationships produce favorable internet evaluations and reviews, which have a big impact on prospective clients. According to a Bright Local poll, 91% of shoppers look up online reviews before making a purchase.

Tough Times : Resilience: - Loyalty During Crises**: Consumers that have a strong bond with a company are more inclined to stick with it through difficult times. Businesses may withstand pressure from the competition and economic downturns with the aid of this resilience.
Supportive Community**: A group of devoted consumers can offer insightful criticism, encourage the introduction of

new products, and aid in a brand's comeback from setbacks.

Sustainable Growth**: - **Lifetime Value**: Creating sincere bonds with clients raises their lifetime value. Long-term engagement, diverse product exploration, and greater purchases are all more likely with them.
- **Organic Growth**: Word-of-mouth and recommendations from happy customers promote organic growth, negating the need for costly marketing initiatives.

ESTABLISHING SINCERE RELATIONSHIP

Creating meaningful, long-lasting links with clients is the goal of developing true connections with them, which go beyond transactional interactions. We will go over more tactics, psychological insights, sophisticated methods, and practical applications in this chapter to help you have a deeper grasp of building genuine relationships with your clients.

The Connection's Psychological Underpinnings

Gaining an understanding of the psychological underpinnings of interpersonal connections can greatly improve your capacity to form sincere relationships.

Mutual Exchange** - **Reciprocity**: According

to this principle, people feel compelled to repay benefits. You can foster a sense of indebtedness in your consumers by offering value and support without expecting quick returns. This will increase the likelihood that they will return the favor with loyalty and referrals.
- **Practical Application**: Provide individualized help, access to unique content, or free resources. These deeds of kindness have the power to strengthen bonds and increase patronage.

2. **Social Proof**: - **Influence of Others**: People frequently heed the advice and behaviors of others, particularly in ambiguous circumstances. Establishing credibility and trust can be achieved by showcasing the positive experiences of previous consumers.
- **Practical Application**: Highlight the favorable experiences of your current clients via case studies, user-generated material, and testimonials. Putting social evidence up and

center helps soothe prospective buyers and improve their impression of your company.

. **Empathy**: - **Knowing and Expressing Feelings**: Empathy is knowing and expressing other people's feelings. Establishing a true understanding of consumers' needs and problems fosters rapport and trust.
- **Application in Practice**: Engage in conversations with empathy and practice active listening. Say things like "I understand how you feel" or "That sounds frustrating; let's find a solution together" to show that you are aware of their feelings and that you comprehend them.

Complex Methods for Establishing Sincere Relationships

1. **Customer Co-Creation**: - **Involving Customers in Development**: Bring customers into the process of developing and refining goods or services. In addition to offering insightful

data, this instills a sense of value and brand loyalty in your customers.
- **Practical Application**: Establish discussion boards, beta test initiatives, or focus groups where clients can offer their opinions and recommendations. To demonstrate that their opinions count, thank them for their contributions and put their work into practice.

2. **Emotional Branding**: - **Connecting on an Emotional Level**: Drawing on the customer's beliefs, goals, and emotions, emotional branding seeks to forge a connection between the brand and its audience.
- **Practical Application**: Develop a brand narrative that appeals to the feelings of your target audience. To emphasize your brand's beliefs, mission, and effect on people's lives, use narrative. Companies that constantly match their messaging to the ideals and goals of their target market, such as Apple and Nike, are masters of emotional branding.

3. **Building Treasured Moments**: - **Specimen-specific and Tailored Exchanges**: Remarkable encounters set your brand apart from the competition and leave a lasting impact. - **Application in Practice**: Make the extra effort to provide distinctive and customized experiences. These could be handwritten messages of appreciation, unexpected presents, or specially designed services. For instance, premium companies frequently offer customized experiences that are tailored to each customer's unique interests.

Practical Uses for Sincere Connections

The Legendary Service of the Ritz-Carlton**: - **Personalized Guest Experience**: The Ritz-Carlton is renowned for its great customer service, where staff members are given the freedom to design unique experiences for visitors. Employees are urged to anticipate and

attend to unspoken wants and wishes.
- **Impact**: This customized strategy creates enduring memories that encourage steadfast allegiance and repeat business. Visitors frequently tell others about their amazing experiences, which helps the brand's reputation grow through word-of-mouth.

The customer engagement strategy of Warby Parker is centered around the customer. The eyeglasses firm interacts with its customers through a variety of channels, such as social media, in-store events, and home try-on programs. Their main goal is to provide customers with a stress-free and delightful experience.
- **Impact**: Warby Parker creates close relationships with customers that encourage loyalty and favorable referrals by actively interacting with them and taking their comments into account when developing new products.

3. **Patagonia's Ethical Commitment**: - **Alignment with Customer Values**: By adhering to ethical business practices and environmental sustainability, Patagonia establishes a connection with its customers. They engage customers in their environmental activities and openly explain their ideals. **Impact**: By being in line with the values of the target audience, a strong emotional bond is created, which develops into a devoted following of supporters and brand ambassadors.

Using Technology to Strengthen Bonds

Customer Relationship Management (CRM) Systems: - **Centralized Customer Data**: CRM programs that store and arrange customer information, such as HubSpot or Salesforce, give users a thorough understanding of their interactions and preferences.
- **Practical Application**: Track customer

interactions, audience segmentation, and personalization of communications with CRM systems. Workflows that are automated can guarantee prompt follow-ups and constant participation.

2. **Chatbots and Artificial Intelligence**: - **24/7 Engagement**: AI-driven chatbots instantly reply to consumer questions, improving the customer experience by providing round-the-clock assistance.
- **Practical Application**: Use chatbots to collect consumer feedback, respond to standard inquiries, and offer tailored recommendations. In addition to improving customer happiness, this technology frees up human agents for more intricate conversations.

3. **Social Media Platforms**: - **Direct Customer Interaction**: Direct and instantaneous customer interaction is made possible by social media platforms. These

platforms allow brands to interact with consumers, answer questions, and foster a sense of community.

Practical Application: Use social media to actively interact with your audience by leaving comments, posting content created by users, and holding Q&A or live streaming sessions. Your brand's relationship with its audience can be strengthened via regular, sincere social media involvement.

Assessing the Effect of Sincere Relationships

1. **Net Promoter Score (NPS) and Customer Satisfaction**: - **Satisfaction Metrics**: Use surveys and feedback forms to track customer satisfaction on a regular basis. NPS may show you whether or not consumers are inclined to tell others about your brand.
- **Practical Application**: Monitor the success of your relationship-building initiatives over time by using customer satisfaction and NPS scores to pinpoint areas that need work.

2. **Retention Metrics**: - **Customer Retention and Churn Rates**: To determine how long your customer connections will last, track your churn and retention rates.

- **Application in Practice**: Put tactics in place to increase retention that are based on measurements for satisfaction and feedback. In order to lower attrition and increase loyalty, take immediate, proactive action on challenges.

3. **Interaction and Engagement Metrics**: - **Engagement Rates**: Monitor metrics like website engagement, social media interactions, and email open rates to determine how well you are interacting with your audience.
- **Practical Application**: Use engagement data analysis to improve the content and strategy of your communications. High engagement rates are a sign of your audience's interest and strong connections.

CHAPTER THREE

Creating Your Value Proposition

In the cutthroat world of sales, differentiating yourself with a compelling value proposition is essential to drawing in clients. The core of what sets your product or service apart from the competition and convinces customers to choose you over them is your value proposition. Creating a value offer that is appealing, succinct, and easy to understand can make all the difference in gaining or losing a transaction. This chapter will examine the components of a compelling value proposition, strategies for developing one, and practical examples that highlight its effectiveness.

A Strong Value Proposition's Components

A compelling value proposition consists of a number of essential components. Gaining an understanding of and incorporating these components will enable you to craft a proposition that appeals to your intended audience.

Simple and Clear Language**: Your value proposition should be simple to comprehend. Steer clear of technical terms and jargon that could confuse prospective clients. Quick Understanding**: Make sure that your value proposition is clear in a matter of seconds. Customers that are busy should understand what you offer and why it's advantageous right away.

Specificity- Concrete Benefits** : Describe in detail the particular advantages that your good or service offers. Whenever feasible, replace generalizations with specific examples and numerical data.
Specimen Features**: Emphasize the distinctive features of your offering. Describe how your offering addresses issues or enhances current solutions.

Relevance, Customer-Centric**: Your value offer ought to cater to the particular requirements, preferences, and issues that your intended audience faces. It need to be pertinent to their goals and experiences.
Personalization: To increase the impact of your value proposition, tailor it as much as you can to the needs of **various clientele groups.**

Credibility or Proof Points**: Provide evidence to support your statements, such as statistics, case studies, and recommendations. Establishing credibility is crucial for gaining the confidence of doubtful clients.
Warranties and Guarantees: By lowering perceived risk, providing warranties or guarantees can strengthen your value proposition.

The fifth point is Differentiation or Distinct Positioning: Clearly state how your good or service is superior to and different from that of the competitors. It should be clear from your value offer why they should pick you.
Competitive Advantage: Emphasize your distinct

advantages and strengths that make it hard for rivals to match.

Methods for Formulating an Enticing Value Proposition

1. **Customer Research and Insights**: - **Customer Surveys and Interviews**: Ask your customers directly through surveys and interviews in order to get their input. Recognize their preferences, wants, and areas of discomfort. Tools such as Google Forms and SurveyMonkey can help with this procedure.
- **Personas of Customers**: Make thorough customer personas that accurately reflect the various target consumer groupings. Psychographics, behavioral attributes, and demographics should all be included in these personas.

2. **Competitive Analysis** - **Competitor Benchmarking**: Examine the value propositions of your rivals to find weaknesses and possibilities. Examine their advantages and disadvantages to determine where you can set yourself apart.
- **SWOT Analysis**: To comprehend your competitive position and pinpoint unique selling features, conduct a SWOT analysis (Strengths, Weaknesses, Opportunities, and Threats).

3. **Benefits vs. Features**: - **Highlight Benefits**: Don't just list features; concentrate on the advantages your product or service offers. Benefits answer the question, "what's in it for me?" from the viewpoint of the client.
Mapping of Features and Benefits: Make a feature-benefit map that associates every element of your product

with a particular advantage. This task makes it clearer how your features add value for the user.

Emotional Appeal: - **Connect Emotionally**: Develop your value proposition to speak to both the cognitive and emotional requirements of your target audience. Purchasing decisions can be strongly influenced by emotional ties.
- **Storytelling**: To communicate your value proposition, use storytelling. Your proposition might become more memorable and accessible with the help of an engaging tale.

Testing and Improvement**: - **A/B Testing**: Examine several iterations of your value proposition using A/B testing. This makes it easier to determine which language, structure, or message most appeals to your target demographic.
Continuous Improvement: Evaluate and improve your value proposition on a regular basis in response to market developments and consumer input. A value proposition should adapt to the shifting needs of your company and the market.
Examples of Successful Value Propositions in the Real World

Apple's iPhone :Simple and Elegant: Simultaneous integration, elegance, and simplicity are at the core of Apple's value proposition for the iPhone. "The best iPhone ever" places a strong emphasis on innovation and ongoing development.
Customer Experience : Apple emphasizes characteristics like design, performance, and ecosystem integration, with a

focus on the total user experience. The takeaway is unmistakable: having an iPhone means enjoying an exceptional and hassle-free experience.

Productivity and Collaboration: Slack's value proposition is "Be More Productive at Work with Less Effort." This is the communication platform offered by Slack. This speaks directly to the necessity of effective teamwork and communication in the workplace.
- **User-Friendly Interface**: Slack is a vital center for workplace communication because it places a strong emphasis on usability and integration with other products. Their proposal emphasizes how Slack lessens email clutter and streamlines work.

Convenience and Cost Savings: The value proposition of Dollar Shave Club is "A Great Shave for a Few Bucks a Month." This focuses on how affordable their razors are and how convenient subscription-based delivery is.
*Humor and Relatability**: They employ comedy in their marketing to engage consumers and create a memorable and relatable brand. The proposal places a strong emphasis on hassle-free shaving at an affordable price.

Developing a Unique Value Proposition

Find Your Core Value**: - **Value Exploration**: Consider what really adds value to your product or service. Think about the issues it resolves, the advantages it provides, and the distinctive qualities it offers the market.

Core Message**: Condense this value into a concise, understandable core message. The core of your value proposition need to be this message.

Activate Your Group**: - **Group Brainstorming**: Include your group in the creation of your value proposition. Diverse viewpoints can yield insightful observations and creative concepts.
- **Input by Cross-Department**: Consult with several departments, including product development, marketing, sales, and customer service. Every team has a different perspective on what appeals to customers.

Develop and Refine - First Draft: Based on your research and idea generation, develop a first version of your value proposition. Make sure it is distinct, believable, relevant, clear, and detailed.
- **Feedback Loop**: Send the draft to a few chosen customers and internal stakeholders for comments. Utilize their suggestions to enhance and strengthen your value offer.

Effective Communication - Consistent Messaging: Make sure that your value proposition is conveyed in a consistent manner via all customer interactions and marketing platforms. This covers your advertising, sales materials, social media accounts, and website.
Visual and Verbal Elements**: To enhance your spoken content, include visual elements like pictures, info graphics, and videos. Your value offer can be communicated more successfully with the use of visuals.
Developing an appealing value proposition necessitates a thorough comprehension of your product and your target

market. In addition to the previously covered fundamental components, there exist supplementary tactics and perspectives that can enhance your value proposition and make it genuinely appealing to your target audience.

Knowing the psychological and emotional factors that influence consumer behavior is essential. Emotional considerations frequently influence purchasing decisions, even while rational benefits like cost savings and efficiency are considerable. Brands may establish a deeper bond with their audience by appealing to feelings like security, happiness, and pride. For instance, in order to appeal to people's emotional desire for security and stability, insurance companies frequently highlight protection for loved ones and peace of mind.

One of the best ways to improve your value proposition is through storytelling. You may make your proposal more relatable and interesting by enclosing it in a gripping story. Narratives of actual clients who have benefited from your product or service can provide a concrete and memorable example of its worth. These customer stories should emphasize problems they had and how your product solved them, making the advantages more relatable and tangible.

Concentrating on the benefits and outcomes your product offers rather than merely its features is another smart tactic. Consumers are more concerned with how your product will benefit their companies or way of life. Your value offer will stand out if it emphasizes benefits like improved well-being, more productivity, or higher profitability. Success stories and case studies can be especially helpful in illustrating these results and provide tangible evidence to support your assertions.

When creating your value proposition, it's also critical to take the various phases of the client journey into account. While potential clients in the decision-making stage may require more precise, in-depth material that answers their worries and objections, those in the awareness stage may be searching for high-level advantages and reasons to think about your product. Your value proposition might be stronger and more convincing if it is customized for each of these phases.

Another important component in differentiating your unique proposition is personalization. You can target distinct audience segments with your message by utilizing facts and insights about your clientele. Value propositions that are tailored to an individual's needs and preferences will be more appealing and relevant. An e-commerce platform might, for example, emphasize cost reductions and offers for budget-conscious customers while highlighting ease of use and convenience for busy professionals.

Adding social evidence to your value argument can make it much more credible. Testimonials, endorsements, reviews, and user-generated material are examples of social proof that demonstrate other people have had success with your product. This can boost trust and lower perceived risk, increasing the likelihood that potential buyers will select your product. Emphasizing the support of prominent figures or industry professionals will increase your reputation even more.

Your value proposition can be strengthened by utilizing visual components. Your message can be communicated more successfully with infographics, films, and pictures than it can with just text. You may convey complicated ideas more effectively by using visual content, which is frequently more interesting and simpler to understand. An infographic that highlights the salient characteristics and advantages of your product, for instance, can help people understand and remember your value proposition.

It is imperative that you periodically review and improve your value proposition because the competition landscape is ever-changing. Technological developments, consumer tastes, and market trends can all affect how successful your message is. You can stay ahead of these changes and make sure your value proposition is still engaging and relevant by regularly conducting consumer research and competitive analysis.

A/B testing various iterations of your value proposition can yield insightful data on what appeals to your target audience the most. Your value proposition can be improved over time by identifying the most effective components through experimentation with various messages, formats, and images. You can optimize the effect of your message and improve iteratively with its assistance.

Enhancing your value proposition can also be achieved through departmental collaboration. Diverse viewpoints and ideas can be brought to the table by involving team members from product development, sales, marketing, and customer service. distinct departments have distinct ways of interacting with consumers, and each can provide special insights into what customers value and how best to convey those values.

In the end, a strong value proposition is a guarantee to your clients about the exceptional value you provide, not just a declaration. It ought to serve as the cornerstone of all your sales and marketing initiatives, conveyed consistently through all media and touchpoints. A well-crafted value proposition can help you stand out from the competition, draw in and keep clients, and promote long-term success.

When creating your value proposition, keep in mind that it is a dynamic component of your business plan rather than a fixed one. Your value proposition should evolve as your company expands and markets shift in order to satisfy changing consumer demands. You can make sure your value proposition stays a potent weapon in your sales and marketing toolbox by consistently asking for input, keeping an eye on industry developments, and honing your messaging.

CHAPTER FOUR

Strategies for Effective Communication

Good communication is essential to a successful sales strategy. It serves as a link between your value proposition and your target market, assisting in the communication of the special advantages of your good or service in a way that appeals to them and motivates them to take action. This chapter will cover a number of techniques to improve your communication abilities and make sure the content you convey is understandable, interesting, and captivating.

Recognizing the Basis of Powerful Communication

Effective sales communication is really about starting a conversation that develops rapport, establishes trust, and answers requirements. It goes beyond simply conveying information. The following fundamental ideas are important to think about:

- **Clarity**: Make sure your message is understandable and unambiguous. Steer clear of vagueness, convoluted terminology, and jargon.
- **Consistency**: Make sure your messaging is the same over all touchpoints and mediums. This reduces confusion and helps create a consistent brand image.
- **Empathy**: Recognize and respond to the feelings and viewpoints of others who are watching you. Demonstrate

your compassion for their wants and needs.
- **Active Listening**: Two-way communication is necessary. Take note of the input from your clients and give considerate answers.

Formulating Your Text

Your message has to be customized for your target audience, highlighting their unique requirements, tastes, and problems. How to write an engaging message is as follows:

Know Your Audience**: Recognize the characteristics, interests, and driving forces of your clientele. Make use of consumer personas to direct your message.
Value-Focused**: Emphasize the advantages and worth that your good or service offers. Describe how it makes the customer's life better or solves difficulties.
Emotional Appeal** : Appeal to your audience's feelings. Emotional ties can motivate participation, whether they are motivated by security, contentment, or pride.
Storytelling**: Tell tales to help you explain your points. Compared to plain statistics, narratives are more relevant and memorable. Tell use-case examples or customer success stories.

Techniques for Verbal Communication

Your message's efficacy can be greatly impacted by how you present it. The following verbal communication strategies will improve the way you connect with others:

Tone and Pace: Speak in an upbeat, confident, and

energetic manner. Modify your tempo to guarantee comprehension and involvement.
- **Ask inquiries**: Use open-ended inquiries to pique the interest of your audience. This promotes communication and sheds light on their preferences and wants.
- **Paraphrasing**: State what your client says again using your own terminology. This helps them make their views clear and demonstrates that you are listening.
- **Summarize and Confirm**: To make sure everyone is understanding and in agreement, summarize the main themes of the discussion.

Nonverbal Exchanges

Nonverbal clues can establish connection and support your message. Be mindful of:

- **Body Language**: Continue to project a smile and be approachable. To establish trust, make eye contact and use gestures to highlight points.
- **Facial Expressions**: Make sure your expressions convey the same meaning. A smile can communicate friendliness and kindness.
- **stance**: Confident stance helps convey legitimacy and authority. Steer clear of protective or closed stances, such as crossed arms.
- **Proximity**: Respect others' personal space, but when it's appropriate, use proximity to foster a feeling of closeness and connection.

Written correspondence

Written communication is just as crucial as vocal

communication in the digital age. Here's how to write messages that are effective:

1. **Email Communication**: Use attention-grabbing subject lines, personalize emails, and send brief messages. Emphasize the main advantages and provide a clear call to action.
2. **Content Marketing**: Produce informative and interesting content for your audience. Whitepapers, case studies, and blog entries can help you become recognized as a thinking leader.
3. **Social Media**: Engage your audience through social media sites. Participate in discussions, exchange pertinent content, and answer comments.
4. **Proposals and Presentations**: Make sure your proposals are organized, concise, and targeted at the needs of the client. To improve your message, include images.

Utilizing Technology

With the use of technology, you can improve communication by giving people more engaging and interactive tools. Take a look at these tech tools:

Customer Relationship Management (CRM) Systems: CRM systems facilitate the management of customer contacts, the keeping of communication logs, and the personalization of subsequent contacts.
- **Email Marketing Platforms**: You can automate email campaigns and monitor engagement metrics using tools like Mailchimp or Constant Contact.
- **Video Conferencing**: Even from a distance, in-person conversations are made possible by programs like Zoom or

Microsoft Teams. Make virtual presentations and meetings with these tools.
- **Social Media Tools**: Programs like Buffer or Hootsuite can be used to schedule and manage social media posts, monitor interaction, and assess results.

Establishing Credibility and Trust

The goal of effective communication is to establish credibility and trust in addition to conveying a message. Here's how to build and preserve confidence:

Transparency: Communicate in an honest and open manner. Admit errors and take quick action to resolve problems.
Consistency : Send messages that are the same over all channels. Confusion and a decline in confidence might result from inconsistencies.
Reliability** : Keep your word and fulfill your obligations. Establishing long-lasting partnerships requires reliability.
Authenticity**: Show sincerity in all of your communications. Authenticity increases relatability and builds trust for your brand.

Breaking Through Communication Obstacles

Effective engagement might be hampered by impediments to communication. Here's how to get over typical obstacles:

Language Barriers: Steer clear of jargon and speak plainly. If necessary, think about translating things for non-native speakers.
- **Differences in Culture**: Recognize cultural variations

and modify your communication approach appropriately. Honor cultural customs and traditions.
Technological Challenges: Make sure the people you communicate with can access and comprehend the technologies you utilize. If required, offer resources and assistance.
- **Perceptual Barriers**: Clearly state any preconceived notions and biases. To dispel unfavorable opinions, communicate in a straightforward and fact-based manner.

Assessing the Efficiency of Communication

You should monitor and assess the results of your communication tactics to make sure they are working. Here's how to go about doing it:

1. **Customer Feedback**: Ask customers about their experiences interacting with your brand on a regular basis. To obtain information, conduct evaluations, interviews, and surveys.
2. **Engagement Metrics** : To determine efficacy and interest, monitor engagement metrics like open rates, click-through rates, and social media engagements.
3. **Conversion Rates**: Calculate how well your communications are converting. High conversion rates show that people are responding to your communications and taking action.
4. **Customer Retention**: Keep an eye on your customers' retention rates to gauge how well your communication tactics are working over time. Retained clients recommend meaningful and productive exchanges.

Ongoing Enhancement

continual improvement is necessary for effective communication, which is a continual process. Keep abreast with the most recent developments in technologies, strategies, and communication. Review and improve your communication tactics on a regular basis in light of performance statistics and comments. To promote creativity and advancement, cultivate an environment of candid communication among your team members.

CHAPTER FIVE

Using Psychology to Improve Sales

In the field of sales, knowing the psychological concepts that influence human behavior can be quite useful. Salespeople may create strategies that connect with their clients more deeply by utilizing these concepts, which will increase engagement, build trust, and eventually increase conversions. This chapter will examine a variety of psychological strategies and how to use them to improve sales results.

The Persuasion Psychology

Robert Cialdini's "Influence: The Psychology of Persuasion" is one of the key books for comprehending the psychology of sales. Cialdini lists six fundamental persuasion ideas that have the potential to be very successful in sales.

1. **Reciprocity**: - **Give to Receive**: According to this concept, people feel compelled to repay kindnesses or favors. In sales, giving out something of value, such a sample, free trial, or helpful information, might make the consumer feel obligated to return the favor by making a purchase.
- **Example**: A lot of software providers provide free trials for their goods. Users are more likely to buy the product to keep getting its benefits after they have put time and effort into using it.

2. **Commitment and Consistency**: - **Foot-in-the-Door Technique**: Individuals generally want to perform consistently. Get clients to commit to a small amount up front, and you increase the likelihood that they will eventually agree to greater requests. This approach is referred to as "foot in the door."
- **Example**: A salesman could ask a prospective client to subscribe to a newsletter beforehand. When they do, they might be more receptive to the idea of a thorough product demonstration or purchase.

3. **Social Proof**: - **The Bandwagon Effect**: Social proof is the propensity for people, particularly in ambiguous circumstances, to seek to others to guide their own behavior. Demonstrating how other people are using and profiting from your product may encourage potential buyers to do the same.
- **Example**: Putting customer reviews, case studies, and testimonials front and center on your website helps reassure prospective customers that there is a high level of trust and value for your product.

4. **Authority**: - **Expert Endorsements**: Individuals who are regarded as authorities or experts in a particular field have a greater chance of persuading others. Using reputable experts' endorsements can increase the credibility of your product.
- **Example**: To vouch for the efficacy of their goods, a skincare company may publish testimonials from dermatologists or other beauty specialists.

5. **Liking**: - **Building Relationships**: People who they like have a greater chance of influencing them.

Customers are more likely to make a purchase when you establish a nice, personable relationship with them and build rapport.
- **Example**: Salespeople can build deeper relationships and achieve more success in the marketplace by taking the time to learn about the needs, interests, and preferences of their clients and interacting with them in a polite and courteous manner.

6. **Scarcity**: - **Creating Urgency**: According to the theory of scarcity, people are more likely to take action when they believe a resource is scarce. Emphasizing time-limited deals or stocks that are limited can instill a sense of urgency that encourages quicker decision-making.
- **Example**: To entice customers to buy right away, e-commerce websites frequently utilize countdown timers for sales or notify users when there are only a few things left in stock.

Sales Emotional Triggers

Emotions frequently have a greater influence on decisions made by people than reason. Salespeople can craft a story that is more engaging and convincing by utilizing emotional cues.

- **FOMO**: The fear of missing out on something can be a strong incentive. It can be more persuasive to emphasize what consumers stand to lose by doing nothing than what they will gain by doing. One way to increase urgency is to highlight the possible drawbacks of not using a product, such as missing out on opportunities or lagging behind competitors.

- **Desire for Belonging**: Belonging to a group and feeling like a part of it is a basic human urge. It can be rather effective to market your product as a means of gaining access to a desirable neighborhood or way of life. For example, premium brands frequently market a lifestyle and status symbol to their clients in addition to a product.

- **Happiness and Pleasure**: Your product may look more appealing if you connect it to feelings of happiness, contentment, or pleasure. Positive associations can be made via advertising campaigns that use happy imagery, such as pictures of happy consumers using your product.

Anxiety and Fear: Anxiety can be a powerful motivator, but it's not always suitable. Action might be sparked by drawing attention to possible risks or hazards that your product can reduce. This is frequently observed in sectors like insurance and health and safety goods.

Sales and Cognitive Biases

Cognitive biases are consistent patterns of judgmental rationality or divergence from the norm that can be used to improve sales strategies:

Anchoring Bias: When making judgments, people tend to depend a lot on the information they are given first (the anchor). Offering a discount after establishing a high starting price can help the final price look more appealing.

Confirmation Bias: People have a propensity to look for, consider, and retain data that supports their beliefs.

Making your pitch fit the customer's preexisting values and beliefs will help your message come across as more persuasive.

Loss Aversion: Negative results typically make people more sensitive than positive ones. It can be more successful to emphasize what the buyer stands to lose by not buying your product than to emphasize what they will gain.

- **The Decoy Effect**: The preferred alternative may appear more enticing when a third, less appealing option is presented. If you have two pricing plans, for example, adding a third, less advantageous plan may encourage clients to choose the middle- or higher-priced option.

The Endowment Effect: Just because someone owns something, they tend to appreciate it more. Giving away samples or free trials can increase a customer's sense of ownership and increase the likelihood that they will make a purchase.

Real-World Uses and Approaches

1. **Personalized Communication**: You may greatly increase engagement by using data to customize your messaging to each customer's unique interests and habits. Customization demonstrates to clients that you are aware of their particular demands and are taking steps to meet them.

2. **Creating Captivating Visuals**: Text alone frequently lacks the impact that visual content does. To clarify your arguments and increase the recall value of your message, use pictures, infographics, and videos. Visuals can clarify

difficult information and arouse feelings.

3. **Telling Stories**: People find stories interesting and memorable by nature. Tell a compelling story about your product's benefits by including relatable client endorsements and success stories. Your product can become more intriguing and relatable with a well-written tale.

4. **Social Proof and Testimonials**: Make sure your marketing materials include social proof. To establish credibility and trust, emphasize user testimonials, case studies, and good reviews. The comments of people who have used your product well are more likely to be believed by the public.

5. **Exclusivity and Limited-Time Offers**: Make use of scarcity to instill a sense of urgency. Customers may be prompted to act swiftly with countdown timers, exclusive specials, and limited-time offerings. Customers that experience exclusivity may feel appreciated and special, which increases the possibility that they will make a purchase.

6. **Developing Rapport**: Take the time to establish sincere bonds with your clients. Get to know them, their likes, and their problems, then interact with them personally. Purchase decisions can be greatly influenced by rapport and trust.

Case Studies and Practical Illustrations

1. **Amazon Prime Membership**: With their Prime

membership scheme, Amazon makes use of the reciprocity principle. Amazon fosters a sense of value in its customers by providing free shipping, exclusive offers, and extra services. This motivates customers to reciprocate by increasing their purchasing.

2. **Apple's Product Launches**: When introducing new products, Apple skillfully employs social proof and scarcity. A limited supply of the newest iPhone at launch intensifies the sense of urgency, and media images and stories of people waiting in line to purchase them offer potent social evidence.

3. **TOMS Shoes**: With their "One for One" promotion, TOMS donates a pair of shoes to a person in need for each pair of shoes purchased, drawing on social proof and emotional reactions. This builds a deep emotional bond and a great brand image in addition to appealing to customers' compassion.

4. **Netflix's Free Trial**: By providing a free trial, Netflix capitalizes on the endowment effect. Customers are more likely to subscribe to keep access to the service if they realize its worth and convenience.

CHAPTER SIX
Managing Disagreements with Self-Assurance

An essential skill in the sales process is handling objections. Any sales interaction will inevitably include objections, and how you handle them can either help you win the sale or lose it. This chapter will discuss confident objection handling tactics that are supported by tried-and-true methods and psychological understanding.

Recognizing the Types of Objections

When prospective clients are hesitant or have reservations about your good or service, objections occur. These worries fall into a few different categories:

Price**: "It's just too costly."
Value**: "I fail to see the advantages."
Need**: "At this time, I don't need it."
Belief**: "I'm not sure if I'll be able to use this."
Time** : "I have to give it some thought."

Developing a focused and successful response requires an understanding of the underlying cause of an objection.

Getting Ready for Reluctance

To boldly address criticisms, preparation is essential. Prepare your response ahead of time to frequent objections. This enables you to successfully address issues and maintain your composure during the talk.

**Research and Knowledge: Have a deep understanding of your product. Understand its attributes, advantages, and any disadvantages. Know who your rivals are and how your product stacks up.
Customer Insight: Recognize the requirements, problems, and driving forces of your clients. This enables you to customize your answers to address their particular issues.
Practice: To get experience addressing objections, role-play with mentors or coworkers. This boosts your self-assurance and sharpens your reflexes.

Using Empathy and Active Listening

It's important to actively listen to customers' objections and answer in a way that shows empathy. This demonstrates your appreciation for their worries and your sincere desire to find solutions.

- **Listen Without Interrupting**: Give the client time to completely voice their issues before answering. They may feel undervalued and unheard if you interrupt them.
- **Acknowledge and Validate**: Express understanding by expressing that you are aware of their problem. Say things like, "That's a valid concern," or "I understand why you might feel that way."
- **Explain and Probe**: To find the source of the objection, pose follow-up queries. This aids in identifying the fundamental problem and finding a workable solution.

Methods for Dealing with Objects

You can address concerns with confidence and effectiveness by using a few tried-and-true strategies:

The **Felt, Found, Feel Method**:
- **Feel**: Show compassion for the client. "I recognize your feelings."
- **Felt**: Address their worry by pointing out that others have had similar emotions. "Many of our clients have experienced similar feelings."
- **Found**: Offer a resolution based on what has been found by others. "What they discovered is that, ultimately, our product saves them money."

The Method of Boomerang:
- Make the objection a justification for purchasing. For instance, you may reply, "I know it's an investment, but consider the long-term savings and value you'll receive," to a consumer who responds, "It's too expensive."

The Compensation Method
- Acknowledge the criticism and then provide a benefit to offset it. "It is true that our product costs more, but peace of mind is ensured by the lifetime warranty and round-the-clock customer support."

The Comparative Method
- To emphasize your product's distinct value, contrast it with that of your rivals. "I understand that you are concerned about the cost, but our product has more features and provides better customer support than [competitor] does."

The Reverse Method
- Redirect the objection by posing a query to the client. Why do you think it's too costly? Is it being compared to a particular feature?"

Developing Credibility and Trust

A key element in overcoming obstacles is trust. Customers must have faith in your goods to fulfill its promises. Developing trust entails:

Transparency**: Tell the truth about the strengths and weaknesses of your product. Building expectations too high and meeting them too low can erode trust and cause discontent.
Case Studies and Testimonials: Present proof of happy clients who overcame comparable obstacles and discovered benefits from your offering.
Demonstrations and Trials: Provide free trials or product demonstrations so that clients may see the advantages for themselves.
**Credentials and Endorsements: Emphasize any honors, certifications, or recommendations from reliable sources.

Principles of Psychology in Managing Objections

Using psychological concepts can improve your capacity to deal with objections:

Reciprocity: Provide something of value, like a discount, a free trial, or more details. Customers may feel obligated to proceed with the purchase in return as a result

of this.
Scarcity: To generate a sense of urgency, draw attention to limited-time deals or restricted supply. Customers may be inspired to act swiftly in order to take advantage of this.
Authority: Establish yourself as a leading authority in your industry. Talk about what you know and have done to establish credibility and trust.
Social Proof: Show that other people have successfully used your product to overcome comparable concerns by using case studies, reviews, and testimonials.

Real-World Illustrations

The Pricing Objections of Tesla:
- Salespeople frequently use the long-term fuel and maintenance savings, along with the good environmental impact, to offset the initial investment when prospective buyers complain to the high price of Tesla automobiles.

The Value Proposition of Apple **:
Apple responds to criticism of its expensive goods by highlighting their excellent performance, design, and ecosystem integration. The business also makes advantage of social proof by displaying endorsements and testimonies from pleased clients and IT professionals.

Customer Service at Zappos:
Online shoe store Zappos addresses concerns about internet shopping by providing great customer service and a wide return policy. Customers are reassured that they may shop with confidence and trust is built as a result.

Constant Enhancement

Resolving objections is a continual process that needs to be improved constantly. Ask for consumer input on a regular basis to better grasp their concerns. Examine sales exchanges to find trends and improve your answers. Keep up of market developments and rival tactics to foresee potential new objections and adjust your preparation accordingly.

CHAPTER SEVEN
Developing a Customer-Centric Sales Strategy

A client-centric sales strategy is crucial in today's cutthroat industry for creating enduring bonds and attaining long-term success. Throughout the sales process, this strategy puts the customer at the center of every interaction by concentrating on comprehending their needs, offering individualized solutions, and adding value. With the help of applicable examples and helpful hints, we will explore the fundamentals and tactics of a client-centric sales approach in this chapter.

Recognizing the Client-Centric Approach

The foundation of a client-centric sales strategy is the idea that a company's success is inextricably tied to the happiness and prosperity of its clients. This concept emphasizes mutual value creation, trust, and empathy while placing a higher priority on long-term relationships than on short-term advantages.

Important Guidelines for Customer-Centric Sales:

Customer Empathy**: Perceiving and feeling what your clients are feeling. Putting yourself in the customer's position can help you better understand their wants, goals, and obstacles. This is known as empathy.

Value Creation**: Putting the customer's needs first rather than just trying to close the deal when developing a product or service. This involves assisting clients in reaching their objectives and resolving issues.

Personalization**: Adapting your strategy to each customer's unique requirements and preferences. Customizing your interactions, solutions, and communications according to customer insights is known as personalization.

Long-Term Relationships**: Giving developing relationships precedence over quick sales. The goal of a client-centric strategy is to foster loyalty and trust, which will result in recommendations and repeat business.

Active Listening: Having sincere discussions with clients to learn about their requirements, worries, and opinions. In addition to ensuring that the client feels heard and appreciated, active listening promotes trust.

Creating a Culture That Is Client-Centric

Establishing a client-centric culture within your company is the first step towards developing a client-centric sales strategy. All organizational levels, from the top down to the front-line salespeople, must be committed to this.

How to Create a Culture That Is Client-Centric:

Leadership Commitment: The leadership team must advocate for the client-centric mindset and show how important it is by acting and speaking accordingly. Leaders should set an example of client-centric behavior and offer the tools and assistance needed to put this strategy into

practice.
Employee Training: Give your sales force the tools necessary to embrace a client-centric strategy. Empathy, active listening, developing relationships, and value-based marketing should be the main topics of training.
Customer Insights: Make an investment in technologies and solutions that offer insightful data about your customers. Customer data can be gathered and analyzed with the use of customer relationship management (CRM) systems, surveys, and feedback channels.
Incentive Alignment : Match performance indicators and rewards to goals that are focused on the client. Instead than focusing only on meeting short-term sales targets, reward sales professionals for establishing long-term connections, client happiness, and loyalty.
Collaborative Environment: Encourage a cooperative atmosphere where many departments cooperate to improve the clientele's experience. For a smooth and uniform client journey, sales, marketing, customer service, and product development should work together.

How to Put a Client-Centric Sales Approach Into Practice

There are multiple crucial elements involved in implementing a client-centric sales approach, all aimed at improving the customer experience and fostering better relationships.

Do Your Homework and Get to Know Your Customers:
- To better understand your target audience, conduct in-depth research. This covers purchasing patterns, pain areas,

and motivations in addition to demographic data.
- Create thorough consumer personas to represent various audience segments. These personas assist you in customizing your strategy to each segment's unique requirements.

Pay Attention Actively:
- Paying close attention to, comprehending, and reacting to your clients is known as active listening. It demonstrates your appreciation for their opinions and your dedication to meeting their demands.
Ask open-ended questions to entice clients to express their opinions and worries. For instance, "Could you elaborate on the difficulties you're having using your present solution?"

Customize Your Method:
Customization extends beyond only utilizing the client's name. It entails tailoring your interactions, messages, and solutions to the unique requirements and preferences of the client.
Utilize the data acquired from active listening and consumer research to customize your follow-up messages, product recommendations, and sales presentation.

Pay Attention to Value Creation:
- Put more emphasis on providing value to customers and resolving issues rather than just selling items. This entails learning about the objectives of the client and showcasing how your good or service may support them.
Emphasize the special qualities and advantages of your product that cater to the demands of the target market. To demonstrate the value you can bring, use case studies and

testimonials.

Establish Credibility and Trust:
An essential element of a client-centric sales strategy is trust. Be open, truthful, and dependable in all of your communications with clients.
Give proof of the dependability and efficacy of your product by using case studies, client testimonials, and reputable sources' endorsements.
- Keep your word when you make promises in order to gradually gain reputation and confidence.

Offer Outstanding Client Care:
- A client-centric sales approach's primary differentiation is exceptional customer service. Make sure that each and every touchpoint is a happy one for your customers.
- React quickly to questions and concerns from customers. Go above and beyond to address problems and offer assistance.
- Follow up with clients on a regular basis to find out if they are happy with their purchases and to take care of any lingering issues.

Seek and Consider Input**:
- Actively seek out consumer feedback in order to comprehend their viewpoints and pinpoint areas in need of development. To obtain information, use feedback forms, interviews, and surveys.
- Take the suggestions made in order to enhance your offerings in terms of goods and services as well as your sales procedure. Demonstrate to clients that you appreciate their feedback and are dedicated to ongoing development.

Assess and Evaluate Client Satisfaction**:
- Put measurements and tools in place to monitor client satisfaction and the effectiveness of your client-centric sales strategy. Customer satisfaction ratings, Net Promoter Scores (NPS), and customer retention rates are a few examples of key performance indicators (KPIs).
- Consistently examine the data to find patterns, advantages, and room for development. Make use of these information to improve the consumer experience and your strategy.

Examples of Client-Centric Sales Strategies in the Real World

Amazon
- Amazon is well known for its customer-focused philosophy. The corporation's motto, "Earth's most customer-centric company," is embodied in the flawless shopping experience, tailored suggestions, and top-notch customer support offered by Amazon.
- Amazon makes sure that customers see products that are relevant to their interests by using customer data to deliver personalized product suggestions. Convenience is also given first priority by the business, which offers quick shipping, simple returns, and attentive customer service.

**Zappos
- The online shoe retailer Zappos has established a client-centric brand. The organization places a high value on providing outstanding customer service and strives to "wow" clients at every turn.
- Zappos gives customers the confidence to shop by providing a generous refund policy together with free

shipping and returns. The organization gives its customer support agents the freedom to go above and beyond in order to satisfy clients and fix problems.

Salesforce
- Leading CRM platform Salesforce highlights the significance of comprehending and meeting customer needs. The company's emphasis on customer success is a reflection of its client-centric methodology.
Salesforce offers a variety of tools, such as training courses, customer success managers, and support services, to assist clients in reaching their objectives. High levels of client satisfaction and loyalty can be attributed to the company's dedication to their success.

Apple**:
- Apple's emphasis on developing cutting-edge goods that improve the consumer experience is indicative of its client-centric business strategy. The company prioritizes customer support, design, and usability.
- The Genius Bar in Apple stores offers individualized help, product demonstrations, and technical support.
Additionally, the business leverages client feedback to keep refining its offerings.

A Client-Centric Sales Approach's Advantages

There are several advantages to using a client-centric sales approach, including:

Enhanced Customer happiness**: You may increase customer happiness and loyalty by putting the needs of your customers first and offering tailored solutions.

Higher Customer Retention**: Repeat business and customer loyalty from happy customers increase the likelihood that they will stick with your business.
Good Word-of-Mouth**: Contented consumers are more inclined to refer people to your product or service, which generates good word-of-mouth and referrals.
Difference from Competitors: Your business can stand out from rivals who might be more concerned with achieving quick sales than establishing lasting connections by adopting a client-centric strategy.
Enhanced Sales Performance**: You raise your chances of closing deals and attaining better sales performance by establishing credibility and adding value.
Enhanced Brand Reputation**: A positive brand reputation draws in more business and cultivates loyalty. It is a result of a dedication to customer success and satisfaction.

Obstacles and Things to Think About

Although a client-centric sales technique has many advantages, there are drawbacks as well:

Allocation of Resources**: Adopting a client-centric strategy could call for more time, money, expertise, and technological resources.
**Balancing Short-Term and Long-Term Goals: It can be difficult to find the ideal balance between meeting short-term sales goals and fostering long-term connections.
Consistency Across Channels**: It's critical to guarantee a uniform client experience at all points of contact, including online, in-person, and via customer support.
Changing with the Needs of the Customer**: Over time, the needs and preferences of the customer change.

Maintaining awareness of these developments and modifying your strategy are essential for sustained success.

CHAPTER EIGHT

The Value of Further Investigation

Following up with a prospect can be the difference between closing a transaction and losing them in the sales process. Many sales professionals undervalue or perform follow-up inconsistently, despite its crucial significance. In addition to helping close deals, a well-implemented follow-up plan fosters enduring connections and guarantees client pleasure. This chapter will examine the value of follow-up, supported by facts and useful advice, and offer tips and tactics for improving your follow-up procedure.

Recognizing the Importance of Follow-Up

After an initial interaction, follow-up refers to the process of staying in touch with both existing and new customers. It accomplishes a number of important goals:

Maintaining Engagement: Follow-up keeps the dialogue flowing, keeping prospects interested and ensuring they don't forget about your offer.
Establishing connections**: Establishing trust and demonstrating your worth for the client through consistent follow-up is essential to establishing enduring connections.
Addressing Concerns**: By giving you the chance to address any reservations or objections the customer may have, you can improve the chances of completing the deal.

Demonstrating Commitment: By following up, you differentiate yourself from rivals who might not be as attentive and show that you are committed to the demands and satisfaction of the consumer.
Feedback Collection: By collecting input on your goods or services, you may enhance them and better serve your clientele.
Cross-Selling and Upselling: Additional needs and chances for cross-selling or upselling may be found through follow-up.

How Follow-Up Affects Sales Success

Research repeatedly demonstrates that follow-up is essential to successful sales:

Several Touchpoints**: Research indicates that converting a prospect into a customer requires an average of five to seven touchpoints. The absence of follow-up results in the missed touchpoints.
Persistence Pays Off**: According to a Brevet survey, 44% of salespeople abandon up after just one follow-up call, despite the fact that 80% of sales require five follow-up calls following the initial meeting.
Customer Expectation: According to research published in the Harvard Business Review, businesses that follow up on online leads within an hour are seven times more likely to have productive discussions with important decision-makers than those that wait until an hour later.

Different Follow-Up Methods

There are various ways to follow up, and they all have

different functions and stages in the sales process:

First Follow-Up: This happens soon after the initial meeting with a potential client with the goal of maintaining the momentum and answering any pressing concerns.
Scheduled Follow-Up: Follow-ups that are prearranged and scheduled to happen at predetermined intervals, like following a product demonstration, proposal submission, or trial period.
Check-In Follow-Up: Consistent follow-ups to keep the connection going and offer support even in the absence of a direct sales opportunity.
Feedback Follow-Up: Following up with a consumer to inquire about their experience and level of satisfaction.
Special Occasion Follow-Up: Reaching out to clients on important days such as holidays, anniversaries, or birthdays in order to express gratitude and remain in their minds.

The Best Methods for Successful Follow-Up

Think about the following best practices to increase the efficacy of your follow-up strategy:

Timeliness**: After the initial contact, follow up as soon as possible. Your chances of keeping the prospect interested increase with the promptness of your follow-up.
Personalization**: Tailor your follow-up correspondence to the particular requirements, interests, and past exchanges of the prospect. Make your messages relevant and interesting by using their name and bringing up previous discussions.
Value Addition**: Make sure the prospect gains something from each follow-up. Provide them with helpful resources,

insights, or information that meets their requirements and enables them to make wise decisions.

** Consistency**: Keep a regular follow-up schedule without becoming overly confrontational. It's important to strike the correct balance between patience and perseverance.

Various Channels**: When following up, use a variety of channels of communication, including social media, phone calls, email, and in-person meetings. Different channels may be preferred by different prospects.

Clear Purpose: A call to action and a clear purpose should be included in every follow-up. Make your goals clear, whether you're setting up a meeting, responding to a query, or offering further details.

CRM Utilization**: Make effective use of Customer Relationship Management (CRM) technologies to monitor interactions, schedule follow-up tasks, and create reminders.

Feedback and Adaptation: Ask for feedback on your follow-up strategy on a regular basis and make adjustments based on what resonates most with your prospects and clients.

Overcoming Typical Obstacles in Follow-Up

Although follow-up is crucial, there may be issues that arise that must be resolved:

**Fear of Rejection: Fear of rejection is a common reason why sellers put off following up. It's critical to reframe rejection as a necessary step in the sales process and a chance to grow.

Time management**: It can be difficult to juggle follow-up

with other sales-related tasks. Use CRM tools and prioritize follow-up tasks to maintain efficiency and organization.
Persistence vs. Annoyance: It's important to know when to give up and when to press on. Pay close attention to the prospect's response and modify the frequency of your follow-ups as necessary.
Content Creation**: It can take a lot of effort to provide insightful and captivating content for follow-up correspondence. To expedite this process, create a library of information that includes articles, case studies, and product manuals.
Practical Illustrations of Successful Follow-Up

Hubble
- Leading CRM software HubSpot stresses the value of prompt and customized follow-up. In order to make sure that leads receive pertinent material and follow-up emails based on their interactions and behaviors, the organization uses automated workflows.
- HubSpot's sales team can increase engagement and conversion rates by customizing follow-up communications to each prospect's unique requirements and interests by utilizing CRM data.

**Zendesk
- Customer support software provider Zendesk sends tailored emails to potential customers quickly after product demos, summarizing the main advantages that are pertinent to their industry.
- This follow-up strategy motivates prospects to proceed with the purchase process by reiterating the benefits of Zendesk's products.

Salesforce **:
- Salesforce uses social media, phone calls, and email as part of a multi-channel follow-up strategy. To ensure prompt engagement, the company's sales personnel are trained to follow up with leads within 24 hours after their initial contact.
- To make follow-up emails more memorable and engaging for prospects, Salesforce also inserts bespoke video messages.

AWS (Amazon Web Services)**:
- After prospects have viewed webinars or downloaded whitepapers, AWS follows up with them via customized emails offering more resources and asking them to set up a meeting with a sales representative.
This strategy offers potential for greater engagement and useful material to assist AWS nurture prospects and advance them down the sales funnel.

The Long-Term Advantages of Regular Follow-Up

Many long-term advantages result from consistent follow-up for salespeople and companies alike:

Enhanced Customer Relationships**: Consistent follow-up fosters deeper, more trustworthy connections with clients, which increases adherence and repeat business.
Improved Customer Retention: Organizations can lower attrition rates and boost customer retention by remaining in touch with clients and anticipating their needs.
Increased Sales Conversion Rates**: Proactive follow-up raises the probability that leads will become clients, which boosts revenue growth and sales conversion rates.

Positive Reputation**: A thorough follow-up procedure shows professionalism and dedication, which improves the company's standing and image.
Valuable Insights**: Product development and marketing plans are informed by follow-up interactions, which yield insightful information about client preferences, pain issues, and feedback.

CHAPTER NINE

Creating Advocates Out of Clients

Creating brand ambassadors out of customers is the ultimate goal of any effective sales approach. Customers who are so happy with your good or service that they gladly and enthusiastically recommend it to others are known as advocates. This chapter examines the methods and advantages of developing client advocates, with the use of practical examples and insightful analysis.

Comprehending Client Advocacy

Beyond just being satisfied customers, client advocacy include clients actively supporting and advertising your company to their networks. Advocates are extremely useful resources because their sincere endorsements are more persuasive than any advertising strategy.

Essential Qualities of Client Advocates

Loyalty**: Advocates have a strong sense of brand loyalty and are inclined to stick with you in the long run.
Engagement**: They are actively involved with your brand; they frequently attend events, offer comments, and keep up with your offerings.
Promotion**: Proponents voluntarily tell others about their good experiences, which affects their purchasing choices.

Constructive Feedback: They offer frank criticism and insights to help you enhance your products and better serve customers.

Reasons to Support Client Advocacy

Enhanced Referrals**: Through word-of-mouth recommendations, advocates are a potent source of referrals that bring in new business.
Enhanced reliability**: Advocates' positive recommendations increase the reliability and dependability of your brand.
Decreased Marketing Costs**: Because advocates assist promote your business, less intensive marketing is required.
Increased Customer Retention**: Advocates have a lower propensity to defect to rival businesses, which results in increased customer retention rates.
important Insights: Advocates offer insightful commentary and important input that can inform marketing plans and product development.

How to Make Your Clients Become Champions

Provide Extraordinary Benefits
Providing outstanding value on a regular basis is the cornerstone of client advocacy. Make sure your offering both fulfills and surpasses the expectations of your customers.
Real-World Example: By continuously exceeding user expectations with innovative, high-quality products, Apple has won over a large number of customers and transformed them into advocates. Through social media and word-of-mouth, Apple products are actively promoted by the brand's

devoted consumer base.

Establish Robust Connections
- Trust and loyalty are fostered by developing close, personal relationships with clients. Spend some time learning about their requirements, inclinations, and difficulties.
Real-World Example: Online shoe store Zappos is renowned for its top-notch customer support and solid client relationships. Numerous clients have become ardent supporters as a result of the business's emphasis on developing personal relationships.

Deliver Exceptional Client Care
- Gaining customers' advocacy requires providing them with exceptional customer service. Make certain that your support staff is prompt, considerate, and proactive in addressing problems.
- Actual Example: The Ritz-Carlton Hotel Company is known for providing exceptional customer service. Employees are encouraged to go above and beyond to satisfy the needs of visitors, resulting in unique experiences that win over patrons into devoted supporters.

Engage Customers Frequently
Frequent interaction builds the relationship and maintains your brand at the forefront of consumers' minds. To stay in touch with your clientele, use events, social media, and newsletters.
Real-World Example: HubSpot regularly hosts webinars, newsletters, and community events to engage its clientele. Through regular interaction, clients become advocates and a sense of community is fostered.

Ask for and respond to feedback
- Actively seek out customer input and apply it to future developments. Loyalty and advocacy are fostered by demonstrating that you value and act upon their ideas.
Real-World Example: Starbucks frequently uses social media and surveys to get input from its patrons. By utilizing these comments to improve services and client experiences, the business builds a devoted following of patrons who act as brand ambassadors.

Establish a Program for Client Advocacy
Establish a structured program for client advocacy that rewards and honors advocates. Give praise, awards, and access to special content as a way to express your gratitude.
Real-World Example: A lot of people became advocates for Dropbox thanks to its referral program. Dropbox provided extra storage space in exchange for referrals, which encouraged customers to tell their networks about the service.

Tell Client Success Stories
Emphasize and commemorate customer victories. Highlight the ways in which your offering has assisted customers in reaching their objectives.
Real-World Example: Salesforce showcases customer success stories at events and on their website. These testimonials highlight the benefits of Salesforce's products and inspire other customers to share their satisfying encounters.

Encourage a Community
- Create a community where customers may interact,

exchange stories, and gain knowledge from one another. Loyalty and advocacy are fostered by a sense of belonging. Real-World Example: Through gatherings, clubs, and internet discussion boards, Harley-Davidson has built a robust riding community. This network makes riders feel like they belong and makes them ardent brand ambassadors.

Make Use of Social Proof
- Showcase client advocacy with case studies, reviews, and testimonials. Credibility is increased and others are inspired to become advocates via social proof.
- Real-World Example: On product pages, Amazon prominently features user reviews. Advocacy reviews that are positive have an impact on other customers' purchase decisions.

Real-World Client Advocacy Experiences

Tesla
Thanks to its cutting-edge products and first-rate customer service, Tesla has been able to convert a large number of its consumers into evangelists. Without using traditional advertising, Tesla owners frequently recommend friends and family and post about their great experiences on social media, which helps the brand grow.

Host Airbnb
The main factor behind Airbnb's success is customer advocacy. Positive experiences are widely shared online by hosts and guests, creating social proof and drawing in new users. In order to promote advocacy and loyalty, Airbnb also interacts with the community through events and

activities.

**Warby Parker
- Warby Parker, an eyewear manufacturer, has amassed a devoted following by emphasizing social impact and customer experience. Numerous consumers have become brand ambassadors, urging others to try on the company's spectacles thanks to its "Home Try-On" initiative and pledge to donate a pair for each pair sold.

Slack
- Slack is a collaboration platform with a robust community of supporters who use social media and word-of-mouth marketing to push the product. Slack has a devoted user community that actively promotes the platform thanks to its emphasis on the user experience, frequent upgrades, and prompt customer service.

Formulating a Long-Term Advocacy Plan

It takes consistency and dedication to quality to turn clients into advocates. The following crucial tactics will guarantee long-term success:

Consistent Quality**: Uphold a high degree of excellence in all of your client contacts, services, and goods. Being consistent strengthens advocacy and fosters trust.
Employee Education**: Educate staff members on how to provide outstanding customer service and the value of client advocacy. Give them the freedom to go above and beyond for customers.
Transparent Communication**: Talk to clients honestly

and freely. Openness fosters trust and motivates customers to act as advocates.

**Recognition and Rewards: Consistently thank advocates for their support and advancement. Express gratitude via special deals, occasions, and public acknowledgement.
Innovation and Improvement**: Constantly invent and enhance your products in response to customer input. Reiterating a dedication to progress strengthens advocacy and allegiance.

Assessing the Effects of Customer Advocacy

Track important indicators like the following to determine how well your client advocacy efforts are working:

**Net Promoter Score (NPS): Indicates how likely customers are to suggest your brand and how loyal they are to it.
Referral Rates**: Monitors the quantity of new customers brought on by recommendations from current advocates.
Customer Lifetime Value (CLV)**: Calculates the total amount of money a customer has brought in during the course of their engagement with your business.
Engagement Metrics**: Monitors how much participation there is in your community projects, events, and advocacy activities.
Reviews and Testimonials: Examines the quantity and tone of customer reviews, testimonials, and feedback.

CHAPTER TEN

Sales Improvement That Never Stops

The one constant in the fast-paced world of sales is change. Salespeople must embrace continual improvement since markets change, consumer preferences change, and new technology arise. This chapter explores the idea of ongoing sales improvement and offers comprehensive tactics, practical examples, and useful insights to keep you on top of the game.

The Constant Need for Sales Improvement

Continuous improvement, which is frequently linked to the Japanese idea of "Kaizen," entails gradually improving procedures, end products, and overall performance over time. This entails continuously improving your methods, approaches, and resources in sales in order to get superior outcomes. A number of variables make ongoing improvement necessary:

Adapting to Changing Customer Expectations**: Modern consumers have higher expectations and are better informed. They expect value-driven interactions, prompt responses, and personalized experiences.
Competitive Environment**: Given the heightened competition, losing market share can result from inaction. You can keep your competitive advantage by making

constant improvements.
Technological Developments**: The sales process can be completely transformed by new technology. Accepting these innovations can increase productivity and simplify processes.
Market Dynamics**: Sales teams must quickly adjust to changes in the economy, regulations, and industry trends. Making constant improvements guarantees that you are equipped to handle these adjustments.
Feedback and Learning: Learning and growth are made possible by routinely evaluating performance and taking feedback into account. This improves sales results.

Techniques for Ongoing Enhancement

Frequent Education and Training
- Continual training is essential for keeping sales personnel abreast of emerging methodologies and market trends. To improve abilities, make regular investments in webinars, workshops, and courses.
- Real-World Example: HubSpot gives salespeople access to ongoing training via HubSpot Academy, which equips them with the most recent information and certifications in inbound sales, CRM utilization, and other areas.

Accept Automation and Technology: Using technology can improve data management, expedite sales operations, and improve customer relations. AI-driven analytics, sales automation software, and CRM systems are examples of useful tools.
Actual As an illustration, Salesforce tracks client contacts, automates repetitive activities, and provides actionable information using its own CRM platform, freeing up sales

people to concentrate on fostering relationships and closing deals.

Establish a mechanism for routinely gathering and reviewing customer and sales team input in order to implement a feedback loop. Utilize these comments to pinpoint areas that need work and make the necessary adjustments.
Actual As an illustration, Amazon significantly depends on user input to improve its sales tactics. To improve its product offers and customer service, the business constantly examines reviews and comments from customers.

Establish Specific, Measurable Objectives and Key Performance Indicators (KPIs) - Establish KPIs that will allow you to monitor your progress and pinpoint areas that require improvement. Make sure these measurements are consistently in line with your overall goals by reviewing them.
Actual As an illustration, the sales teams at Google establish explicit quarterly goals and key results (OKRs), which are then routinely assessed to make sure they are on track and require any necessary revisions.

Promote a Culture of Learning: Encourage an environment that values growth and learning. Honor and commend team members that go above and beyond to improve their abilities and streamline procedures.
Actual Example: By providing employees with access to LinkedIn Learning, a platform featuring an extensive library of courses on sales skills, industry trends, and personal development, LinkedIn encourages a culture of

learning.

Analyze and Improve Sales Processes: To reduce inefficiencies and boost effectiveness, evaluate and improve sales processes on a regular basis. To find areas that need optimization and bottlenecks, use data-driven insights.
Actual Example: To find opportunities for improvement, Microsoft regularly evaluates its sales processes using information from its CRM and other tools. Workflows are now more effective, and sales performance has increased as a result.

Leverage Data and Analytics: Make use of data analytics to learn about market trends, sales performance, and customer behavior. Utilize these insights to customise sales strategies and make well-informed judgments.
Actual As an illustration, Netflix uses data analytics to comprehend the tastes and actions of its users. Their sales methods are informed by this data-driven strategy, which also enables them to tailor advice and marketing initiatives.

Promote Collaboration and Communication: Promote a cooperative atmosphere wherein members of the sales team exchange tactics, insights, and best practices. Innovative solutions might result from regular brainstorming sessions and team meetings.
- Actual Example: To efficiently communicate, Slack's sales teams use their own communication tool. Their culture of open communication enables them to collaborate and exchange ideas to enhance sales procedures.

Adopt a Customer-Centric Approach: Continually hone

your sales strategy to put the wants and preferences of the customer first. Customize your communications and interactions to add value and foster enduring connections.
- Example from Real Life: Nordstrom is well known for its customer-focused sales strategy. By concentrating on delivering outstanding customer experiences, Nordstrom has amassed a devoted following of patrons who promote the company.

Track Market Developments and Rivals**: - Keep yourself updated about developments in the market and rivalry. This knowledge aids in anticipating changes and modifying your tactics to maintain your competitive edge.
- Real-World Example: Coca-Cola keeps a close eye on rivalry and market trends. They can develop and maintain their lead in the fiercely competitive beverage sector thanks to this proactive strategy.

Overcoming Obstacles in Constant Enhancement

Resistance to Change: One frequent obstacle is resistance to change. To combat this, make sure team members understand the advantages of ongoing development and are included in the decision-making process.
- Actual For instance: IBM encountered opposition when they introduced a new CRM system. Through staff participation in the planning process and thorough training, they overcome resistance and increased sales productivity.

Time and Resource Restraints: Initiatives for continuous improvement may require a lot of time and resources. Assign resources to projects in accordance with their prospective impact and prioritize them.

Real-World Example: A tiny company might not have a lot of resources available for ongoing development. They can still make a big difference if they concentrate on high-impact areas like streamlining customer communications or automating tedious jobs.

Preserving Consistency: Consistency is essential to ongoing development. Create procedures and systems that guarantee regular evaluation, criticism, and improvement execution. Actual Example: Toyota's constant implementation of continuous improvement ideas is credited with its success with Kaizen. Productivity and quality have steadily improved as a result of ongoing evaluations and small adjustments.

Measuring Impact: It can be difficult to gauge the success of initiatives for continuous improvement. To be sure that improvements are producing the expected results, establish precise measurements and evaluate progress on a regular basis.
Actual Example: To make sure that changes are in line with overarching business objectives, GE measures the effectiveness of its continuous improvement programs using a combination of financial and operational metrics.

Examples of Continuous Improvement in the Real World

Toyota: By putting Kaizen into practice, Toyota is a leader in continuous improvement. All staff members are encouraged to provide suggestions for enhancements, which results in advances in customer service, quality assurance, and manufacturing.

For instance, assembly line workers at Toyota frequently recommend minor adjustments that boost productivity and cut waste. Toyota's philosophy of constant development has elevated the company to the top of the automotive sector.

Procter & Gamble (P&G): P&G uses continuous improvement to boost creativity and productivity in its production and product development operations. The "Connect + Develop" initiative of the corporation promotes cooperation with outside partners in order to boost innovation.
As an illustration, P&G's constant innovation efforts have produced products like Tide Pods, which transformed the laundry detergent industry by giving customers a handy, pre-measured option.

General Electric (GE): GE uses Six Sigma techniques to increase quality and efficiency throughout its operations, demonstrating its dedication to continuous improvement. The organization has significantly reduced costs and improved performance as a result of its focus on data-driven changes.
- As an illustration, GE Aviation implemented Six Sigma to enhance the aviation engine manufacturing process, which decreased production costs, decreased defects, and raised customer satisfaction.

Amazon - Amazon's emphasis on innovation and customer passion fuels its culture of constant development. The organization is always looking for methods to improve customer satisfaction and expedite processes.
As an illustration, consider how Amazon's use of AI and

machine learning to streamline its logistics and supply chain has sped up delivery times, enhanced inventory control, and raised customer happiness.

The ability to adjust and continuously improve is becoming necessary in the quickly changing field of sales. The essential elements of contemporary sales have been covered in this book, from developing compelling value propositions and using psychology to truly connecting with customers to comprehending them and understanding them. You now have all of the information and resources needed to succeed in a cutthroat industry thanks to each chapter. But the path starts with the unwavering pursuit of excellence and doesn't finish with knowledge alone.

The Importance of Ongoing Development

Adopting a mindset that embraces change, innovation, and growth is key to continuous improvement in the sales process. It's about realizing that there's always space for improvement, regardless of your level of expertise or achievement. This strategy guarantees that you constantly meet and surpass the expectations of your clients, keeping you one step ahead of the competition.

There are numerous advantages to constant improvement:

- **Adaptability**: Continuous improvement keeps you flexible and responsive in a world where market dynamics and consumer tastes are ever-changing.
- **Customer Loyalty**: You may create extraordinary experiences and value for your consumers, converting them into devoted champions, by continuously improving your sales methods and procedures.
- **Operational Efficiency**: Increasing productivity and

efficiency via the use of technology and process streamlining frees up time to concentrate on developing connections and closing sales.
- **Innovative Edge**: Adapting to new concepts and technologies helps you differentiate yourself from rivals by keeping your sales approach novel and creative.

Adopting a Customer-Centric Perspective

Understanding and providing for your customers is the foundation of ongoing improvement. This is paying attention to what they need, getting their input, and adjusting your sales strategy based on what you learn. A customer-centric approach fosters word-of-mouth recommendations, long-term success, and the development of trust and loyalty.

- **Active Listening**: Talk to your clients, elicit questions from them, and pay attention to their opinions. This gives them a sense of value and hearing, in addition to assisting you in understanding their requirements.
Personalization: Make use of data and insights to customize offers and interactions, offering each client individualized solutions that speak to them.
- **Proactive Problem Solving**: Foresee possible problems and take proactive measures to resolve them. This demonstrates to them your concern for their experience and dedication to their pleasure.

Utilizing Data and Technology

Continuous improvement requires integrating technology and data analytics into your sales approach. These tools help you make wise decisions and maximize your strategy by giving you insightful information about market trends, sales performance, and customer behavior.

- **CRM Systems**: Track sales activity, handle customer interactions, and analyze data to make better decisions by using Customer Relationship Management (CRM) systems.
- **Sales Automation**: To boost productivity and free up your sales team to work on high-value tasks, automate repetitive processes like reporting, data input, and follow-ups.
- **Data Analytics**: Use data analytics to learn about performance indicators, sales patterns, and customer preferences. Make greater use of this knowledge to hone your tactics and achieve desired outcomes.

Fostering an Innovative and Learning Culture

Maintaining a culture of creativity and constant learning within your sales staff is crucial to long-term success. Motivate your group to be open to new concepts, look for educational opportunities, and never stop trying to get better.

Ongoing Training: To keep your personnel abreast of the most recent advancements in the field and sales strategies, allocate funds into frequent training and development initiatives.
- **Collaborative Environment**: Encourage team members to work together and share information. Frequent feedback loops and brainstorming sessions can provide creative solutions and best practices.
- **Recognition and Rewards**: Give team members

credit for their contributions to ongoing efforts at improvement. This serves to both inspire people and emphasize the value of continuous improvement.

The Path of Constant Enhancement

As your sales career progresses, never forget that ongoing development is a process rather than a final goal. It calls for commitment, resiliency, and an openness to change. your book's tactics and insights are intended to provide you the tools you need to succeed on your trip.

Adhering to a continuous improvement mindset will help you expand your business sustainably, cultivate a culture of excellence within your team, and forge enduring relationships with your clients in addition to increasing your sales success.

Accept the ideas of continual development and allow them to lead you to achieve greater success in your sales profession. Recall that the secret to being an expert in the art of selling is to be flexible, creative, and relentless in your pursuit of greatness. Even though the route may be difficult, the benefits are definitely worth the effort. Remain inquisitive, steadfast, and always growing. Your achievement is only getting started.

www.ingramcontent.com/pod-product-compliance
Lightning Source LLC
Chambersburg PA
CBHW050319230526
45471CB00005B/2256